To my family, friends, and past lovers. Thank you for the unconditional love, and support. Thank you for loving me despite my flaws and mistakes. For wiping the tears that create rivers and lakes. This is for you.

SC

MY MISTAKES AND YOU

AUSTIN MACAULEY PUBLISHERS™

LONDON ✶ CAMBRIDGE ✶ NEW YORK ✶ SHARJAH

Ordering Information
Quantity sales: Special discounts are available on quantity purchases by corporations, associations, and others. For details, contact the publisher at the address below.

Publisher's Cataloging-in-Publication data
SC
My Mistakes and You

ISBN 9798889105503 (Paperback)
ISBN 9798889105510 (ePub e-book)

Library of Congress Control Number: 2023920679

www.austinmacauley.com/us

First Published 2024
Austin Macauley Publishers LLC
40 Wall Street, 33rd Floor, Suite 3302
New York, NY 10005
USA

mail-usa@austinmacauley.com
+1 (646) 5125767

I would like to thank Jennifer Cardenas for coming up
with the cover illustration.

Table of Contents

We are flawed, broken, beautiful, one of a kind, and we make mistakes. So take a deep breath, open a bottle of wine, turn on the TV, and cry your heart out. I'll be here crying with you.

To him, I don't quite understand how you were able to make me feel like the luckiest girl in the world but at the same time make me feel like the most miserable person. I still love you and that's my mistake.

I Am Leaving

I just want you to know I love you
I really do
But I just wanted you to know
Even if it seems like I don't

I want to love and be loved
But how can I love someone
When I don't love myself,
I am stuck in this antagonizing hell

I feel trapped in a love unsure what to do
I don't love myself the way I love you
I am not even sure what that is or means
So I think it is best I leave

What I want to say is I am sorry
But I am leaving
Because you don't need me
Because I know my love is not what you need

I am sorry but this time I chose someone else besides you
I saw the colors you bled, and they weren't true
I am leaving, not for a day, a week, a month, a year, or two
As much time as I need to get over you

Reach You

My mistake is that my words couldn't get through
This time, I will fight until they reach you
They say actions speak louder than words
But my actions have only left you hurt

But you let your actions and words tear me apart
So please don't hate me when I stop loving you this hard
I know it isn't like me to stop without a fight
However breaking has made me lose all my might

I hope this reaches you in time
To know what it really means to live my life
Because the thought of you and me sounded so lovely
I was so sure I'd spend the rest of my life loving you and you only

But I *pray* this reaches you
Because I don't pray to God but I know that you do
You have always lived with this ice around your heart
So this time around, I hope this reaches you from the start

Guys Like Him

Even though I am only nineteen,
The fear of love has finally consumed me
I am afraid to love and be loved
Because not every man is an angel sent from above

I know now how my mother felt
All the pain, and suffering she dealt
To be in love, lost, and confused
Be in love with a man who isn't thinking what will hurt, and break you

I learned what breaks a girl's heart
That she wasn't the only one from the start
What breaks the teenage girls soul
That he wasn't thinking about your heart truth be told

What breaks a mother/woman's will
You weren't enough to satisfy that man's fill
But I know deep down not all men lie and cheat
It just may be before we get to the goods ones all the bad ones we have to
meet

I know we cannot forgive them all
We gave them everything and they chose to let us fall
I want to blame the world for this happening
But *he* broke my heart and that was only the beginning

The saddest part is we are told by our mothers, aunts, cousins, and sisters
Once the love is over, he will leave you cold like a night in winter
So they say run from guys like him
But it's guys like him that know how to fool us in the end

Saving Me

When I left, it was easy to say
But when I left, I went the wrong way
Got emancipated, left the state, and lived on my own
Dropped out of school, and worked myself to the bone

Waiting to hit rock bottom
My demons are catching up, no way to stop them
I've gone bad and there's no saving me
So don't stop and try, just let me be

Concerns I get left and right
But always the same answer, *'I am fine.'*
Once you go that route
There's no saving me, without a doubt

This time, I have really lost myself
Now it's time to put my heart in a box and hide on the shelf
So save your precious energy
I have gone bad, and there is no longer saving me

Too Good to Be the Devil

He was like a flower in a storm
Out of charcoal, he was like a diamond born
I don't know how but had me feeling like this
All it really took was his kiss

He said, 'get too close and you will get burnt.'
Because loving the devil will only get you hurt
But he was a challenge; a man worth the task
Lose yourself, and you can't conquer your path

Like an angel and devil dancing cheek to cheek
The rhythm of our bodies were the only words we could speak
His heart so close but yet so far
But he keeps my heart racing like a speeding car

He's like the angel of small death
Waiting to consume my every last breath
With him, it was like dancing with the devil
I knew what I was doing when I woke on the cold gravel

His words took me to either heaven or hell
And deeper into the underground I fell
I felt he was an angel undercover
A devil who was my lover

And he was too good for his own kind
Angel or devil I didn't care, I didn't mind
He was too good to be underground level
He was too good to be the devil

You

Would you believe me if I told you my darkest secrets
Because these are my mistakes, my weakness
Would you be believe me if I told you, you were the one
Because at the end of the day, you gave me life when I had none

I have made many mistakes
One of them was was to let our friendship get misplaced
I should have apologized for hurting you
But I shut myself out, now my words won't come through

I made my mistakes worse, when I kept you in the dark
I just didn't know if you would understand, it would be hard
Too look you in the eyes and let these dark secrets come out
To let you in and see how badly I let you down

You are my best friend
I hope you can stick through with me to the end
Expressing myself in words is my strength but you already knew
Because I wrote this for you

Flaws

When I lose my patience and I begin to yell,
It seems like I want to cry or laugh you can never tell
I will cuss like a hard ass sailor
But hold me in your lap when I cry later

I have a horrible attitude and unruly hair
But an amazing lover if you are up for the dare
For I am a perfect imperfection,
A person underway mental destruction

So take me for all that I am
Hold me close and keep my heart safe in your hands
Accept me for my flaws and mistakes
Wipe away the tears that can create rivers and lakes

For I have failures, and flaws
But all that I carry with me is great love
I will keep my heart to others out of reach
Be mine and I'll allow you to walk all over me

My flaws will be the reason for my ruined name
Unlike all the other wild horses, I want to be tamed
So wipe away the tears that create rivers and lakes
Love me for my flaws and mistake

Demigod

They said 100 angels were cast from heaven
I always wondered was he one of them
He did things that are beyond human control
I did believe he was too good for this world

But he curses, sins, and bleeds
He certainly is a human being
He isn't the real him but like a fraud
A man of supernatural a Demigod

He was a man that could go to war and come back unhurt
A romantiants but he could easily leave your heart in the dirt
He was so strong, and bold especially with those tattoos
They read histories and tragedies he went through

However, in those two years, he put me through hell
He will never understand the suffering and pain I felt
Even so I always thought so highly of him
He always made everything seem so bright when it was dim

But as always, he let me down
And he never got to hear my heart-breaking cries and sounds
Just when I thought he turned good, he became bad
This why our story never became true which always makes me sad

I hope he remembers the reason why I endured it so much
Because I truly loved him more than such
He was not Superman or a Demi-god
He was just a man who was born a little before me, a man I once loved

Where You Can't See

I know you have carried this burden all alone
This time, I can't let you do this on your own
I want to be the light that comes spilling through the doors
The kind of light that keeps you begging for more

I'll be the light to the places you cannot see
So please this time rely on me
Let me the be light tucked in your pocket
The sort of light of a shooting comet

You will no longer walk in the dark
I will light all the places to reach your heart
So don't carry this burden on your own
Because you are no longer alone

Walk with You

With you, I once felt stronger
I could keep fighting even if it meant a second longer
I became more confident about myself
Able to understand the feelings I once felt

I always wanted to walk with you
Not just side by side but as equals too
Be someone you could rely on
Because it was something you had never done

Along the way, you strayed from your path
Loosened the grip of the hand you once latched
What happened on the day you lost it?
I don't understand how you became like this

Regardless of the fights, no matter the distance
To your problems, I will always be here to listen
I once would of have promised to always be on the road for you
Now you are *no longer* the one I would choose

I still wonder what were you you were doing on the day you lost it
What became the true downfall for our split
Because I still have trouble understanding what love is too
But I could have kept walking if I was with you

Move on

When I know, I am ready to move on to let go
You pull me back with those words my heart deeply knows
The ones that make my heart warm, my smile bright
The words that make me forget our stupid fight

But we know it can't always be like this
Once we let those lies leave our lips,
It's back the beginning before we know it
The same fight the same argument

Because love does doesn't require a manual
With you, it seemed like an essential
When will I understand you never cared for how I felt
So I know life will move on like a conveyor belt

Empty Vessels

I have made a mistake, so please forgive me
I've been sleeping with someone different lately
I know I am the one who called the end
I just didn't think you would be okay with just being friends

We aren't making love
It's all over until one of us is done
We are empty vessels
Nothing more but flowers with wilting petals

Just cold bodies put together
Trying to feel a little better
This is my way to ease the pain
I know I have nothing really to gain

Everything feels so empty
When I know, I no longer have you besides me
I don't feel like a human being
All my emotions and responsibilities I am fleeing

Looking for someone who resembles you
This really all I do
Because I am an empty vessel
Trying to be one with my own devil

For I am an empty vessel,
Not looking for anybody to settle
Just looking for the drive
To feel a little bit more alive

Since it was nice not to be alone
To not wait for your name to pop up on my phone
But he's just an empty vessel
Someone like me trying to feel more special

Louis Vuitton

They say the devil wears Prada
He drinks Black Label no top shelf vodka
Can turn to any form any shape
Will come to you as a man or a snake

His voice cutting through like a knife
And he knows how easily he could ruin your life
This devil is so smart and cunning
Unfortunately never intends to stay but to keep running

His lips that touch your skin
That will always ignite the fire within
That voice of his will always reverberates through your body
He could be good but turns bad so suddenly

Still he is a demon that wears name brand
To lure you in, and trap you in his hands
He just wants to mess up your life than he's gone
This kind of devil wears Louis Vuitton

Stubborn

It's my mistake so I will admit
I can be childish and throw a fit
I will be the reason for your anger and constant worry
Although I am stubborn, you won't hear a sorry

Because I am stubborn, allow me to act strong
Let me put a smile when everything is going wrong
I am nothing more but a weakling
Unable to understand what I am feeling

How can I make it not stay this way
Can I make it to see you another day
I am too stubborn to understand what love is
Because I am stubborn, I can't make the pieces in the puzzle fit

I've walked this road before
Let you be the one to walk out the door
Hold back the tears until it's tightly shut
Cry until everything that I hid is out of my gut

It's my mistake I will admit
I am only trying make my puzzle pieces in your life fit
So I will apologize for the constant worry
This time, I won't be stubborn to say sorry

Forecast

I learned nothing in this world
But only to love and get hurt
But the weather continues to remind me of *you*
The forecast may be predict sunny, but its gray skies nothing blue

They predict the weather will be quite warm
But you can be cold, and your shouts loud as a storm
And you are like the wind that comes and goes through my hair
The forecast called for certain things but like you it doesn't play fair

However when I do want cold and gloomy days
It's seems you are like the weather in your own way
Because you cannot predict the forecast that is you
With you it's not warm or sunny, it cloudy gray skies that lost their blue

Easy

The idea of love was always on my mind
I let the walls down and let you inside
I put down the barricades
To make it easy for you to stay

I cried rivers for you
Dropped the closest people to me for you
Did everything that never pleased me
To make everything for you easy

All that I would and did give up
To you was always never enough
You wanted my soul
To the flesh on my bones

But you still walked away
Let our time together go to waste
You gave your all to someone else
Left me all alone in this burning hell

So I promise one day they will learn the truth
They will learn the deception in you
You make it easy for you to stay
Although harder for them to walk away

Mess

My life with you
Was like a cluttered room
My heart a messy entry way
Impossible to enter, hard to stay

A curse in disguise
A relationship full of secrets and lies
A mess of imperfections
That later would become my own destruction

I allowed you to break me until I bleed
To continue to let you make a mess of me
As time goes, your love decreases
Even when I tried to pick up the pieces

I rose my expectations too high
Leaving a mess in my life
I will make a mess of him
To show karma can be a bitch

I thought I belonged with you
But the mess proved it wasn't true
Soon it will be him in distress
Because I will be the cause to the truth in mess

Phase

I saw you go through many phases
I didn't know you had these hidden faces
I was lost and confused
I thought I knew you

But with each phase you become distant
It makes me feel if we have really lost it
Any hopes we had to be friends
But I knew this was the end

As your phases come and go
I don't know you anymore
Because violence has become your new face
And I know this is not just a phase

He Says

He says he loves you
But never seems really true
He says you are the only one
And yet you can't help think what has he really done

He says he can't stay too long, he has somewhere to be
But could it be a lie, could he simply be losing interest in me
He says attending a family event
But never once are you invited

He says he's too busy to see you
It's the same reason why nothing out of the blue
But he calls you at 2 am
He's had a couple of drinks and you know how that ends

He says he didn't have much to drink
But you can see the bottles, wraps, and lines of cocaine next to the sink
Promises it won't happen again
It was for fun, a new trend

He says no more tears will you shed
It was all talk and lies at the end
Maybe just being friends would be better
You knew would never truly end up together

He was good and bad
But he wasn't the guy you wanted your kids to call Dad
Your friends told you and you never listened
Instead believed every word he said

I Learned

It upset me when I learned you had a child with another
How can I compete with your child's mother
It was a stab in the back when I learned you were moving them down
You knew this place was my new home, my new town

It tore my heart at the left corner when I learned you were living with her
I tried to be supportive, but it only left me bitter
A man would step up and take responsibility
Not let me fall in love willingly

It tore my heart at the right corner when I learned you gave her everything I
ever wanted with you
I guess there is only room for one not for two
A coward waits for the moment he has been caught to justify his actions or
surrender
I learned you were never going to choose the girl like me over the girl like
her

It tore my heart completely apart when I learned you married her
How could we get this far and for you to let this occur
At the end of the "relationship", all I did was learn things on my own
I learned loving you really broke my soul

Melody

You were his start and I was his end
You were once his true love, but I was his best friend
But you became the woman he would possibly spend the rest of his life with
While we had two years, your next anniversary to come would mark the fifth

The one his family loved, his family's Melody
While I remained the home wrecker, the half assed parody
Together we built a new home,
One where I would never see, never go

Where you would raise his first child
A new home your baby could grow and run wild
You were his sweet Melody
And I the woman who had no chance to be

Sacrifice

It started with a love that was forbidden
This is a tale of two people and their inevitable end
A heartbreaking poem of all her struggles
Because a man can never put a girl before his own hustle

For all that he did was for her,
To give her the best life and a bright future
He knew of the enemies he would make along the way
He didn't care as long as he had her to stay

Unfortunately, this isn't about the same "her"
Because she was the sacrifice he did for another
For what he did not want her to know,
He was married and had a daughter and kept on the low

His relationship with her was lies
All along it was an affair, a simple sacrifice
Even when he swore wasn't true
That he would leave them and they could start new

Feeling jealous means those people possess something you don't
As she learned raise your expectations too high, you just get hurt
For time after time, it was always the same saying
'Right now is not a good time' for the price she was paying

Now she hopes that he knows it's become too late
He put her and all that he claimed to love at stake
Turned her into a piece of his sacrifice
A sacrifice for others but other her to live a better life

Sex

Your infectious disease
That took something precious from me
Your sinister lies
Cannot be cured from my life

You gave me something I cannot get rid of
Something that does not come from love
Our intertwined bodies came with a price
With you, I was stuck rolling the dice

How am I supposed to live and forget
When now I am infected with your lies and regrets
To leave me in a place for you to never care, to never look
With you, sex was all that it took

Walls

These walls are clear but not easy to see
I am trapped within its transparency
Like a fish in a bowl
Stuck regardless of what corner I go

This was my life with you
Trapped, escaping was something I cannot do
Everything exposed to the other side
Leaving nowhere for me to hide

You left me sad, alone, and with rage
Left me like an animal stuck in a transparent cage
How I wished the roles were reversed
To wonder how these clears walls would serve

Because these walls were clear
Left me barricaded in with fear
I was a prisoner within its transparency
I was crashing into clear walls I could not see

However, one day I will escape
Break free no matter how long it takes
One day, I will be on the other side
No longer barricaded in these clear four walls of your lies

Release Me

I am trying not to look back
As you watch me continue to pack
The life, love, and lies
Release me just this one time

You are begging me to reconsider
But this is for the better
If I stay any longer,
I will only continue to be a bother

Because your name is shackle
Your love is more than I can handle
So please
Release me

A

Being with you felt so free
The bestest friend to me
I know I am a little late
I am sorry for sending our friendship to the grave

In your beautiful green eyes,
I could always confine
Your presence always felt like shelter to me
You always felt like true family

Long beautiful straight hair
Thank you for always being there
I'll always miss our sleepovers
Each time with wild midnight adventures

But my biggest regret my biggest mistake
And I let it put our relationship at stake
And I will never stop apologizing
Because I know the experience can be traumatizing

It took one thoughtless night
For you to be out of my life,
I am sorry for fucking you over
I should have never opened myself to another

Thank you for setting me free
Once the bestest friend to me
I will always live with my sin
One day I hope you will truly forgive them

Burning Bridges

I always wonder how many bridges have I burned
Have I turned numb that's why I no longer feel as hurt
I build a bridge then I burnt it down
Leaving a pile of shiny silver ashes on the ground

It seems the wood just won't hold
This bridge is going to need something much more bold
Don't be upset for this bridge's inevitable destruction
You have been heavily treading without caution

So put down the nails and hammer
This bridge will need something much stronger
They will need titanium, and thick metal wires
Otherwise, these bridges will continue to catch fire

For this, have become the breaking point
These bridges are burning at their joints
Because I have lost my sanity, my control
I won't hesitate to watch this bridge go

I have always fought for you but you never fought for me
I have burned bridges not one, not two, but more than three
Yet you knew it was my flaw, one of my mistakes
I will continue to burn these bridges without any time to waste

With time, I have become okay with burning a bridge or two
Because I burnt it to put some distance between me and you
I know you will always continue to believe I am the one to blame
So continue to watch me burn these bridges without shame

Cannot Stay

You continue you call name
As you hope I will stay
But you know we have reached the end
There is no going back to lovers or friends

We have reached the end of the tunnel
I am starting to find cracks in this glass bubble
It's not strong enough to contain me
Slowly but surely I am setting myself free

Your begging is pointless
Your love has left me restless
Don't call my name
I cannot stay

Open Doors

I am so hung up on the past
Maybe because I was hoping things would actually last
I keep losing myself
I don't know if next time I will be the same without a doubt

So hung up on the future
Will my dreams come true, will be a mother just like her
I know it's time to let go
Be a better person for my kids to know

So hung up on tomorrow
Not sure if I will bring myself or someone else's sorrow
Will my decisions make my sisters proud
Or will I be that person that no longer sticks around

So hung up on the present
I hope soon my father will no longer feel so distant
I am counting down the days for your release
Will it finally put our hearts at ease

So hung up on the past
Because it upsets me how things did not last
I know now what needs to happen
Know yourself and new doors will open

Stars

We were like the stars
We seemed so close but yet so far
So I became the moon
Learning to be away from you

I no longer needed you to shine
Because all that I did was mine
I no longer desired to be a star
On my own, I came this far

I no longer needed your light
Because at the end, I was the only one to put up a fight
We were once like the stars
I learned I was better off alone from the start

Good-bye

I think this was the hardest goodbye
You thought I would remain by your side
But you knew what we had
Had to eventually come to an end

I saw your face in the rearview mirror
I wish you had not been there
Because for a moment I waned
It was almost enough to make me stay

But I knew if I stayed
It would be too late
And the next time
Would become an even harder goodbye

Home

I don't understand how you were attracted to me
Maybe it was the thrill to be with someone who was only seventeen
But it was my mistake for not seeing it as a sign
To love a girl that young you were out of your mind

I understand how a capturer
Can turn into a lover
They know how to play the role
Of a man who wants to be your home

It was my mistake for not seeing the signs sooner
That I was being trapped in a home with my capturer
Who only wanted was to ruin my life
Calling you my home felt like I could die

Bloom

She wasn't like the perfect groomed flowers
Wasn't watered with gentle rain but crashing showers
Constantly was hit with the sun's rays
Stood proud and strong on lonely days

For she always rose tall and bright
No one dared to come and steal her light
She never was a traditional red rose
That girl was a wildflower that only a few people chose

These petals can cut you like blade
The scent of her came and left like a haze
For she deserved to bloom
To be the light in a dark, lonely room

A man came along to promise more than he could compensate
He said he would water her petals and roots to stop the ache
Because he wanted her to bloom at his side
And if so, he wanted her to fade away with him in time

But she let him in, and it was her mistake
That man only nurtured her for his own sake
But she wasn't meant to bloom by his hands
For when she blooms, she is too much for him to withstand

Eleven Years Old

You are only eleven
And already trying to make your way to heaven
We didn't think about what you were going through
We were hurting but so were you

I should of have looked after you better
Maybe call more and send some letters
But I left you when you possibly needed me most
I should have of come back sooner and kept you close

I should of have suffocated you with hugs
Instead I let you face the world of drugs
I should of have spoiled you harder
Not let you pull all nighters

We should have cooked breakfast together
One where the whole family could gather
We should of have danced and took many pictures with funny faces
Not let your mind go to these dark places

I didn't want to believe the idea of death roams your mind
But I didn't think much of it just turned a blind eye
I should've known you had this ache in your heart
The same one that tore this family apart

I am so sorry
I have made the mistake to leave you in a hurry
I will try my hardest to do better
I promise to be the best sister

You are only 11 years old
I don't know what your future may hold
But you already want to die
I am sorry this family broke you apart and left your side

Older Sister

You made me the black sheep of the family
All your achievements, I will always envy
You are the golden child
The perfect older sister with the best smile

However, you carried more than your shoulders could hold
You added more to your already heavy load
You spent more nights worrying about money
Rather than being young, out at parties

You went into debt for the sake of our father
You took responsibility when no one else seemed to bother
With that, your 20s were taken away by jail visits
New obstacles pushing you to your limits

You never heard the word *"thank you"* enough
Went to work and school even when you wanted to give up
Doing whatever you can to keep everyone surviving
I am sorry you had to become the backbone for this family

But when you thought your world was crashing down
Tables were turned and your luck went back around
And I hope these good changes keep happening to you
Because this time around, you deserve to be happy too

Thank you for being my mean older sister
The one who sheltered this family of the worst disasters
I will continue to always be there as your little sister, as your best friend
Because as the maid of honor, I will be on your side till the end

Damaged Goods

They say your character will be the death of you
Because you put yourself in positions others would not do
But that's your heart of pure gold
Fuck those guys not understanding your kind soul

Damaged goods they call you for being the way you are
Just weak men who don't understand the imperfections of your heart
Let them believe what they want
Leaving you will be the mistake their mind will haunt

For the time we spent together,
Gossiping, catching up late at night in diners
I saw the glimmer behind your eyes
My mistake was to let it fade with those men's lies

I know you will never put my mistakes and flaws on the table
Because you understood better than anyone else my trial and error
Remember your beauty and worth for those boys never would
They don't deserve the time, respect, and love of your damaged goods

Gone

What they said is true
I should have stayed away from you
All your lovely words were lies from the start
Like a bullet aiming straight for my heart

Your intentions were not right
Otherwise, why do they stay on my mind
I should have learned from my past mistakes
I just don't know what seems to be at stake

Believe it when I say I am done
I won't be here when the morning comes
No longer will you see my bare back in the early dawn
Because this time, I will be gone

You will be calling out my name
By that time, it will be too late
Because that saying is true
Nothing good comes from men like you

Mother

Mother, they say I am a reflection of you
I tried to do the same things you did too
I wanted to leave, I wanted to grow up fast
While you were trying to make me stay, keep me young, make my childhood last

But as a reflection of you
The same mistakes you made, I went through
Left home at a young age
Fell in love with a man who wasn't mine to take

Relying on myself and on my own
Living as an outcast, my mistake was to think I was all alone
You tried your hardest to make me not take this path
Because you knew the consequences would be the reason for my wrath

Mother, they say I am a reflection of you
Not from the looks but the adventures and troubles you went through
They say you wanted to grow up fast
So you crossed the border, while I moved to away to make my own path

I am looking through a mirror and I see you
I see that I never thanked you enough for all that you do
I never gave you enough credit for all that you endured
So please accept my apology and these words

Sooner

My biggest mistake was not leaving sooner
When I saw it was too late and you chose her,
I watched from afar the home I could ruin
I had so much anger that I could not keep it in

But instead I will pack my things and go
Your love was only for show
I am better off far away
Otherwise freedoms I will never gain

Because it was crazy to believe
That you were mine to keep
I should have left sooner
But I had hoped you would have chosen me over her

Wife

How I deeply pray for a redo
So I can stand at the altar and say, 'I do.'
How I wish for the retrieval of that last text
Because maybe I would be wearing that white dress

However, we have come to an end
There won't be a celebration with our family and friends
It's our turn to say our goodbyes
This time, to truly part with our lives

I wanted you to love me 10 times more than you do now
Make me feel like the best thing you found
But you are an illusion meant to fade away
Nothing more but a firework that can't stay

You really do lie as easily as your breath
That's why the thing you seek is out of reach
Although it was always a lie of kindness,
It only made me want to hate you more and love you less

You continue to make hurtful mistakes
Making your hard work all go to waste
Because your beginning with me finally ends
This time, there won't be no connection not even friends

I wanted you to love me 20 times more fiercely than you do now
Death won't be the reason for your broken vow
How I wish you could understand the way I felt
But this is the kind of pain I could not inflict on someone else

The person I wanted to spend the rest of my life with was you
But we made some mistakes and now there's nothing we can do
Stay too close to someone, you end up not being able to see them at all
For that, they become the reason for your crash, burn, and fall

The distance between us has remained unchanged
That room will continue to play out our endless days
With you and you only, I wanted to share my life
We parted ways, but I still love you the kind of love that makes me want to
be *your* wife

53

My

My mistakes don't seem to end
I lost you and pushed away my closest friends
My problems don't seem to disappear
It seems I will continue living my life in this despair

My heart can longer bear the disappointment
Even since I know I can't keep these moments
My all *in* can't compare to yours
Because I mean heart, mind, and soul

My million cries don't compare to your two times
For I cried out of pain, but you because of your lies
My lost time cannot be given back
Remorse is something you will always lack

My sacrifice was harsh unlike yours
It was always me broken on the floor
My heart and soul cried "save me"
Never meant anything you that's why I remained so lonely

My love was never ending
But it was never enough to satisfy your filling
My mistake was to love you
For your love wasn't true

Mistakes

Life was meant to make mistakes
But mine has made me lose my bestest mates
These mistakes remind me I cannot rewind time
For I have lost the right to stand by your side

When they ask me about you,
I don't know how to react, what to say, or what to do
It was my mistake to always leave you in the dark
I was selfish, and let it break your heart

They will never understand how dope our friendship was
Because we just needed each other not the alcohol or drugs
I let us drift apart that will always be my mistake
For all I did was, hide from you and push you away

It was a mistake to think we could all easily reconcile
Because I did and said some things that were pretty vile
I have always had these scars that I cannot hide
But you loved me for that, that's how you guys are my ride or die

But you were my best friend since seventh grade
I always admired how you easily forgot my mistakes
As if they were nothing to tear us apart
But this mistake is something that cannot be turned into a piece of art

I hope they understand how much they meant to me
So that's why I never told them but wrote it so they have it to read
That I made mistakes but they did too
But the only difference is my mistake made me lose not one but two

And "You"

I wrote this about my mistakes and "*you*"
Because my tears were no longer enough to get through
I thought I was the love *you* could never leave behind
However, it was all mistakes and lies

When I first met *you*, *you* said I had two walls inside of me
These walls that contained my heart that *you* wanted to set free
Who would have known it could never be predicted or planned
Our love was one that no one could ever understand

On this page, I wrote the words I wanted and could never tell *you*
Because there were words I wanted to say but could not amount to
I loved *you* more than I could ever love myself
But that was my mistake for feeling the way I felt

I am *leaving you,* and continue to *burn bridges*
You put me in your *mess*, this *sacrifice*, I hope these *walls* put some distance
You are *too good to be the devil,* that's why I cannot *walk with you*
Thank you to my friends and family who had these *open doors* that allowed
me to *bloom*

In reality, *you* had "rescue me" written all over your face
You needed someone to rely, help you with your mistakes
But you lost me, living without the comfort of your own home
On these lonely nights, I hope your soul continues to roam

I hope these words pierce *you* and their heart
I was finally able to see what I relied on
Mentally, I thought I was ready to leave on a whim
Emotionally, however, I wasn't prepared to be separated from him

However, I got tired of *you* and your cheap tears
They were no longer enough to keep me here
Because there once were two walls inside of me
But it wasn't *you* who set me free

When they close this book, I hope it reaches them and *you* too
Because I wrote this for *you*
But I am reading it to them
My Mistakes *and You* have come to an end

www.ingramcontent.com/pod-product-compliance
Lightning Source LLC
Chambersburg PA
CBHW061642130726
47996CB00003B/1412